Arthur
and the Lost Diary

ISBN 979-11-86701-05-8 14740

Longtail Books

Arthur
and the Lost Diary

For Laurie

Chapter 1

It was a busy afternoon at the library. Lots of people were **wander**ing about, choosing books or doing **research**.

At one table, Sue Ellen was sitting alone. She didn't look up when anyone walked by, nor did she pay any **attention** to passing **conversation**s. She was **concentrating** on writing in her diary.

Dear Diary: The library is a **crowd**ed place today. A lot of my friends are here **working on** school **project**s. Sometimes I think it's funny that I have so many different kinds of friends. I **wonder** sometimes why I'm friends with them and not with other people.

If I could make up some new friends, what kind would I want? Should they be friends who always give me presents or **volunteer** to clean up my room? Or maybe I'd like famous friends who **star** in TV shows or movies. What makes someone a real friend, anyway?

Sue Ellen put down her pen. That was enough for now. She loved having a diary, a special place to write down her **private** thoughts. It wasn't that her ideas were always great or important. But she liked putting the words on paper, where she could look at them.

She closed the diary and **trace**d the **edge** of the **binding** with her finger. Sue Ellen had **design**ed the **cover** herself. My Diary, she had **print**ed **neat**ly with a **sparkle** pen. Underneath, she had added PRIVATE and DO NOT OPEN in large **letter**s.

The library clock **struck** four times, **remind**ing Sue Ellen that it was time to go. She picked up all the books she wanted to **check out** and **pile**d them on her school notebook and diary. She **tuck**ed everything underneath her arm as she walked to the **circulation** desk. She had to **shift** her arm to stay **balance**d, and when she did, her diary **slip**ped out of the pile and fell silently onto the carpet.

Ms. Turner sat at the checkout **counter**, waiting to help people with their books. She smiled when she saw Sue Ellen.

"That's an **impress**ive pile. I see you're going to be reading a lot this week."

"I couldn't **make up my mind**," Sue Ellen **admit**ted. "There were so many good books to choose from."

As Ms. Turner began checking out the books, Sue Ellen **spread** them on the counter.

When she got to the last one, she **expect**ed to see her diary underneath.

But all she saw was her notebook.

Immediately, she **search**ed among the other books.

"Is anything wrong?" asked Ms. Turner.

"No, I don't think . . . Well, yes." Sue Ellen looked around the floor. All she saw were two paper **clip**s and a pencil **erase**r.

"I think I lost something!" she said.

Quickly, she **retrace**d her **step**s to the table where she had been sitting. The diary wasn't there. Where could it have gone? Diaries don't **disappear** like magic. And they don't walk away by themselves.

She **knelt** down and searched under the chairs and tables, pushing aside feet when she had to.

"Excuse me. **Ouch!** Watch my fingers. Coming through."

Sue Ellen searched everywhere she could

My Diary
Private
Do Not Open

remember walking—and also a few places she hadn't. She even looked through the **waste**baskets.

But it was no good. The diary was nowhere to be found.

Chapter 2

Sue Ellen **drag**ged herself back to the **checkout counter**. Her face was red, and her eyes **watery**.

"What's wrong?" asked Ms. Turner, who could see that Sue Ellen was upset.

"I lost my diary. I had it a minute ago. I don't understand. I must have left it here." She **scan**ned the counter again. "But I guess I didn't."

"Books don't get lost in my library," Ms. Turner **assure**d her. "**Describe** it to me."

Sue Ellen took a deep **breath**. "Well, it kind of looks like a book. It has a **shiny** red **leather cover**. Well, at least it looks like leather. And there are some blue **sparkle letter**s that say My Diary. And under that I wrote PRIVATE. DO NOT OPEN."

"That's very **specific**," said Ms. Turner. "It should make our **search** easier. Don't worry— we'll find it. I'll tell everyone on the **staff** to **be on the lookout**."

"Thanks. I guess I'll keep looking myself. I just wish . . ."

Sue Ellen **pause**d because she heard some laughing. It was **exact**ly the kind of sound a girl might make if she was looking at a secret diary.

"I'll be back," she told Ms. Turner.

Sue Ellen **trace**d the sound to the corner, where Francine was **hunch**ed over some pages.

"So that's where it went!" said Sue Ellen.

She **march**ed up to the desk.

"Pretty funny, huh, Francine?"

Francine **nod**ded. "I'll say. Listen to this—"

"I don't have to listen to it," said Sue Ellen. "I wrote it!" She **snatch**ed the book away from Francine.

"Hey!"

"And there's nothing funny about **steal**ing someone's diary. I'm surprised at you, Francine. I thought you were my—" Sue Ellen looked down at the book. It was red, but it didn't have blue sparkle letters. "Hey, this isn't my diary."

"Of course not," said Francine. "It's a **joke** book. What would I be doing with your diary?"

"I don't know. You could have picked it up. It's red and says PRIVATE on it. I had it a minute ago, and now it's gone."

"How **mysterious**," said Francine. "Do you think it was stolen?"

Sue Ellen didn't know what to think. "It was only **valuable** to me. I've been writing in it forever."

"I've never had a diary," said Francine. "What do you write in it?"

"My ideas, what's happened during the day. Private thoughts. It's very important that I find it, Francine. I mean, there's **stuff** in there about everyone."

Francine's eyes opened wide. "Everyone? When you say *everyone*, you mean *everyone?*"

"Yes, yes, but that's not what **matter**s now."

"It matters to me," said Francine. "What have you been writing?"

"I can't talk about that now. I have to find my diary."

Before Francine could say anything more, Sue Ellen **rush**ed off. If she didn't find the diary soon, she didn't know what she would do.

Chapter

3

"What's wrong with Sue Ellen?" Muffy asked Francine.

"She's all upset about losing her diary. It says PRIVATE on the front of it. She even thought I was reading it." Francine shook her head. "I don't see why that would upset her."

"Hmmm," said Muffy. "Maybe she wrote something in it about you—something she doesn't want you to read."

"About me?" Francine put her hands on her **hip**s. "But what would she write about me?"

"Maybe all the **mean** things you've done

to her."

Francine looked surprised. "What things?"

Muffy **fold**ed her arms. "Like pushing her in the **mud** yesterday."

"I did not push her," Francine **insist**ed. "She **trip**ped."

"Right next to you, though."

"I just happened to be there. I don't push people in the mud."

"Well, you laughed."

"Of course, I laughed. It was funny. She was covered with mud."

Muffy **cross**ed her arms. "You were standing next to her when she fell, and you laughed **afterward**. What if she *thinks* you pushed her?"

Francine **bit** her lip.

*She suddenly saw a **beard**ed doctor in a white coat sitting behind a large desk. After a **knock** at the door, Sue Ellen came in. She was **spatter**ed in mud.*

*"Do you have an **appointment**?" asked the doctor.*

*"No," Sue Ellen **admit**ted, "but I have to see you **at once**, Dr. Zimmer. It's an **emergency**."*

*"Ah! And what is the **nature** of this emergency?*

Sue Ellen held out her arms. "Can't you tell? Francine just pushed me in the mud."

*The doctor **stroke**d his beard. "So I see," he said.*

*Sue Ellen **consult**ed her diary. "That's the seventeenth time this month that Francine has been mean to me. Something must be done! I came to you because you're the world's **lead**ing **specialist** in mean children."*

"True, true," said the doctor. "May I see that?" He took the diary from Sue Ellen and looked through it quickly.

*"Ah, yes," he said. "Pushing. Laughing. Eating the fruit **filling** in your **snack** pie and leaving you only the **crust**." He **sigh**ed. "I'm **afraid** your friend **exhibit**s all the **sign**s of **acute** ogre-ism.*"*

"Ogre-ism?"

*"**Exact**ly." The doctor pushed a button on his desk, and a **flicker**ing TV screen **appear**ed on the wall. It showed a girl screaming at other children. Then she pushed one of them down.*

*"As you can see," the doctor continued, "this is a **disease** in which the **victim** cannot control her meanness."*

"That's Francine!"

Dr. Zimmer stopped the film. "We have been watching her for a long time. I'm afraid there's no help for her. We must keep her away from the other children!"

*At that moment Francine **burst** in on them. She **point**ed a finger at Sue Ellen. "I thought I'd find you here!"*

*But before Francine could do anything **further**, two **uniform**ed **guard**s ran in and **restrain**ed her.*

★ **ogre-ism** 오거(Ogre)는 중세 기사 이야기에 등장하는 거인을 말한다. 여기에서는 -ism을 붙여 '아주 못된 행동을 하는 병'이라는 의미로 쓰였다.

"Leave me alone!" Francine shouted.

"Sorry," said one of the guards, "but ogre-ism is very **contagious**. *We must* **remove** *you at once."*

*"**Besides**," said the second guard, "the other children don't want to play with you. You've been too mean to them."*

"But I can change! Really!"

The guards laughed.

"If we had a nickel for every time we heard that one . . . ," said the first guard.*

"We would have a lot of nickels," the second guard finished up.

Then they both laughed again.

★ **nickel** 미국이나 캐나다에서 쓰이는 5센트 동전.

"But you have to give me another chance," said Francine. "I don't have ogre-ism."

"You don't have what?" Muffy asked.

Francine **blink**ed. She was back in the library.

"It's a **disease**. Sue Ellen may have written about it in her diary."

Francine stood up and **wipe**d her **forehead**. "I need a drink."

She **head**ed off for the water **fountain**.

"Francine is so **excitable** sometimes," Muffy said to herself. "Sue Ellen probably didn't write about her at all." She **paused**, **lean**ing against a

shelf. "Of course, she did have to write about something. Everyday events can be so **boring**, though. She probably has to **make up** stories. . . ."

*Muffy saw herself looking into a long mirror. She was dressed as a princess, in a long **flow**ing dress with a **jewel**ed **crown** on her head.*

*Sue Ellen was standing next to her. She was wearing a **plain** dress with no **jewelry**.*

*"Princess Millicenta," said Sue Ellen, "there is no one who **compare**s with you."*

*"**Go on**," said Muffy.*

"You are rich."

"True."

"You are beautiful"

"True again."

"And you are the smartest princess in the land."

"Three for three," Muffy agreed.

*"You are so **fair**," Sue Ellen went on, "while I am just okay."*

*A shadow **hid** the sun for a moment.*

*"Who **dares** to **interrupt** my fine weather?" asked Muffy.*

*Sue Ellen looked out the window and **gasp**ed. "It's a dragon!" she cried. "A fire-**breathing** dragon. And it's causing big trouble in the **village**."*

*Muffy **comb**ed her hair. "What are the villagers doing about it?"*

"They're running this way!"

*"They are?" The princess was **alarm**ed.*

"Help us!" shouted the villagers. "Help us, rich and beautiful and smart Princess Millicenta!"

*Muffy **sigh**ed. "I guess we should do something."*

*"Fear not, princess!" said Sue Ellen, putting on a **suit** of **armor**. "I'll **handle** this!"*

*She started **clank**ing down the tower stairs, but after a few moments, the clanking stopped.*

*"What's the **matter**?" asked Muffy. "Why have you stopped?"*

*"Ooof," Sue Ellen called up. "I'm **stuck** in the*

doorway." She gasped. "And the dragon is approaching!"

Muffy looked out the window. The dragon was on its way up the hill.

Muffy sighed. "If you want something done right, you've got to do it yourself."

She took the end of her long, **braid**ed hair and **thread**ed it through a **handy pulley** outside the window. Then she lowered herself to the ground.

As the dragon **prepare**d to **toast** Sue Ellen to a **crisp**, Muffy **spritz**ed it with a bottle of her **perfume**.

The dragon's fire was **snuff**ed out.

"Oh, princess!" **gush**ed Sue Ellen. "My thanks! I don't know how I can ever **repay** you!"

"Well, this perfume is thirty dollars a bottle. You can start there."

Sue Ellen sighed. "You must be the most **practical** princess in the world."

"Yes," Muffy said happily. "I **suppose** I am."

Chapter 5

"Hey, space cadet!★" said Binky, **tap**ping Muffy on the shoulder.

Muffy **blink**ed. "What's that? You can't talk to me that way. I'm a princess."

Binky just **shrug**ged. "Okay, okay. But whatever you are, you're **block**ing the **shelf**. I need to look for a book back there."

"Oh, sorry." Muffy **step**ped **aside**. "I guess I was thinking about Sue Ellen's diary. She lost it."

★ **space cadet** 멍한 사람 또는 현실과 동떨어진 사람을 가리키는 표현.

"**Tough** luck."

"It had the most wonderful story about me. . . ."

Binky looked **confuse**d. "I thought this was Sue Ellen's diary."

"Well, it is. But a diary is a good place to write about your friends."

"Really?" said Binky. "What did this diary look like?"

"I'm not sure. But it said PRIVATE on it."

"I saw a book like that," said Binky. "It was on the floor. I put it on one of the **cart**s."

"You did?"

Binky **nod**ded. "It's not good to leave books on the floor."

"Did you look inside it?" Muffy asked.

"No," said Binky. "Why would I? The report I'm doing isn't on anything PRIVATE."

"I know, I know," said Muffy. "But that's not the **point**. A diary can be very, um, interesting. People write down how they really feel about everything."

"*Everything?*"

Muffy nodded. "And everybody. I just hope we can find it."

She left to see if she could help with the **search**.

Binky was **impress**ed. "Everybody, huh?" he said to himself. Keeping a diary sounded like a lot of work. Writing one didn't **appeal** to him. But if Sue Ellen was writing about everybody . . .

Binky **reach**ed up to get a book, but his arm **froze** in **midair**.

"That would even **include** me!" he **realize**d.

Binky saw Sue Ellen sitting at a desk in her bedroom. She was writing in her diary.

Dear Diary: Today was very special. I was able to spend almost all my time with Binky Banes, the man of my dreams.

*She **drew** a picture of Binky in the **margin**. He had on sunglasses like a movie star.*

He's so handsome—and strong, too. Today the school bus got **stuck** in the **mud**, and Binky **volunteer**ed to go **lift** up the back end. The bus driver said that wouldn't be **necessary**. But Binky did it anyway, and the driver didn't seem to **mind**.

I can tell that the other boys all **look up to** Binky. Who can **blame** them? I only wish I could get Binky to **notice** me. I try smiling at him a lot, but he only asks me what's wrong with my face. I follow him around on the **playground**, but he wants to know if I'm lost or something. I've even started bringing him extra **dessert**s for lunch. At least that gets his **attention**. And I know he likes the desserts because he always **burps afterward**.

I'm not sure I can **go on**, though, without letting him know how I feel. Maybe tonight I should go over to his house and **serenade** him under his window. If that doesn't show him, nothing will.

34

"What's the **matter**, Binky?" said Arthur. "You look like the Statue of Liberty.★"

"Huh?" Binky **drop**ped his arm like a stone.

Arthur was **load**ed down with the **stack** of books he had picked out. "Are you all right? You look a little **strange**."

"No, no, I'm fine. Don't forget, I can **lift** the back of a bus."

"You can what?"

"Um, **never mind**." Binky wanted to change

★ **Statue of Liberty** 자유의 여신상. 미국 뉴욕항의 리버티섬에 있는 여신상을 가리킨다.

the **subject**. "Did you hear? Sue Ellen lost her diary. I put it on the **cart**."

Arthur **frown**ed. "Why didn't you give it back to her?"

"I didn't know it was her diary then. It was just some book with PRIVATE written across the front."

"PRIVATE?" said Arthur. "I **wonder** why."

Binky **shudder**ed. "You can wonder all you want, but don't **expect** any help from me. I'm done wondering. See you later."

"Bye," said Arthur. He thought Binky was acting a little **odd**. Maybe holding his arm up like that had **cut off** the blood **supply** to his brain.

It was too bad about Sue Ellen's diary. Arthur knew that people didn't always say everything they were thinking in **public**. But in her diary, especially with all that PRIVATE **stuff**, Sue Ellen probably didn't **hold back**.

"Arthur, what are you doing with all those books?"

"Doing?" said Arthur. "I'm planning to take them out."

Sue Ellen looked at the titles. "**Mystery** of the **Mummy**'s **Curse, Eerie Canal**s of Mars.★ Arthur, I can't believe you read this stuff."

"Why not?"

"It's not good for you. Don't you get **nightmare**s?"

"Not from reading," said Arthur "I like **adventure**s."

"Oh, really? Have you had any nightmares in the last week?"

"I—I guess so."

Sue Ellen **fold**ed her arms. "And have you read any of these kinds of books in the last week?"

"Well, yes . . ."

★**Mars** 화성. 지구의 밖을 돌고 있는 첫 번째의 외행성이며, 태양을 중심으로 4번째 궤도를 공전하는 태양계 행성이다.

"I rest my case,*" said Sue Ellen. "You know, Arthur, I've been watching you very closely."

"You have?"

Sue Ellen nodded. "You're not perfect, Arthur. **In fact**, you're wide open for **improve**ment I've **kept track of** your **flaw**s in my diary."

"You shouldn't have gone to all that trouble," said Arthur.

"Oh, it's no trouble," said Sue Ellen. "I keep everything **organize**d in my diary. But I can't just write about these things anymore. I have to **take action**."

"What kind of action?"

"To **shape** you people **up**. I've made a list of the ways you could change."

She took a **scroll** of paper out of her pocket. It unrolled down to her feet and **halfway** across the room.

★**I rest my case** '자, 내가 말한 대로잖아'라는 뜻의 표현. 주로 법정에서 변호사가 자신의 논지를 충분히 입증했다는 의미로 쓰인다.

Arthur
FLAWS
7
8
9
10
11
12
13
14
25
26
27
28
30
31

"'Number 1,'" she read aloud.

*Arthur **sigh**ed. He looked around for a way to escape.*

*Sue Ellen stopped reading. "I know that look. Maybe we should **skip direct**ly to Number 78."*

*Arthur was almost **afraid** to ask. "What's that?" he said finally.*

*Sue Ellen moved along the paper. "'Number 78: Doesn't take **criticism** well.' Now, are you going to sit still? We've got work to do."*

*There didn't seem to be any way out. But as Sue Ellen went **hunt**ing for the top of the list, she moved **slight**ly to one side. Arthur saw his chance—and **dove** through an opening in the book**shelves**.*

Chapter 7

"Hey! **Watch out!**" cried one of the library **assistant**s as Arthur **crash**ed into his cart.

The books went flying.

"Sorry," said Arthur, **pick**ing **himself up** off the floor. "I was trying to . . . Well, **never mind.**"

"Look at this **mess**," said the assistant. He started picking the books up.

"Here, let me help," said Arthur.

The assistant jumped back. "How do I know you won't try to **tackle** me again?"

"I wasn't tackling you," said Arthur. "I was

just trying to escape."

"Escape? Escape from what?"

Arthur **shrug**ged. "It's not important. I'm safe now. So please let me help."

"Okay. But just remember, I've **got my eye on** you."

Arthur began **gather**ing some of the books. They came in all different sizes and **subject**s. One, in **particular**, caught his **attention**. It said PRIVATE on the front.

At the other end of the library, Binky, Muffy, and Francine were **hunt**ing as a team. The girls were looking through the **bookcase**s, checking on the desks and chairs.

Binky was down **on his hands and knees**.

"Here, little diary," he said. "Come out, come out, wherever you are."

Francine **gave** him **a look**. "Do you really think that will help?"

"It can't hurt," Binky **insist**ed.

"The diary shouldn't be that hard to find," said Muffy.

Francine **frown**ed. "**Unless** somebody else has found it first."

Muffy **gasp**ed.

"What's wrong?" Binky and Francine asked together.

"Nothing," said Muffy. "I was just thinking. What if a **big-time** movie **producer** found the diary? She might want to make a movie about it. The movie would be a giant success. Everyone in it would be known all over the world. Wouldn't that be great?"

Francine and Binky **stare**d at each other. "No!" they shouted.

"Look harder," said Francine.

"Much harder," Binky added.

They **renew**ed the **search** as Arthur **came by**.

"Muffy, have you—"

"No questions now, Arthur. Can't you see I'm busy?"

Actually, Arthur had **wonder**ed why Muffy was looking under the seat **cushion**s. He had never seen her do that before.

"I just wanted to know if you've seen Sue Ellen."

"Not for a while."

"Can you—?"

"Do I need to **spell** it out for you, Arthur? I'm *B-U-S-Y*. **Get the message**?"

"Loud and clear."

Arthur moved over to where Francine was **flip**ping **through** some newspapers.

"What about you, Francine?"

"What about me?"

"Have you seen Sue Ellen?"

"Arthur, I'm not **keep**ing **track of** anybody right now. I have a job to do."

"If you could just . . . Whoa! Binky, what are you doing?"

Binky had **lift**ed one of Arthur's feet into the air.

"Just checking," he said. He put Arthur's foot back down.

"Well, **leave** my feet **out of** it. **By the way**, you haven't seen Sue Ellen, have you?"

"I can't see anyone from down here," Binky **admit**ted.

Arthur **scratch**ed his head. "Why are you down there, anyway? Wait, don't tell me. I have to go find Sue Ellen."

"What's so important that you have to find her now?" Muffy asked.

"Oh, I found her diary."

Everyone **froze**.

Chapter 8

Arthur, Muffy, Binky, and Francine sat around the table. Sue Ellen's diary sat in the middle. The word PRIVATE seemed to be **glaring** at them from the **cover**.

Binky **reach**ed for it, but Arthur put his hand on the cover.

"I really don't think we should do this," he said. "I mean, would you want someone to read *your* diary?"

"I don't *have* a diary," said Binky, "so how would *I* know?" Still, he **hesitate**d.

"**Honest**ly, Arthur," said Francine, "don't you

want to know what she wrote about you?"

"Well . . . kind of . . . I guess."

"It's **settled**, then," said Muffy. "Who's going to read first?"

Francine and Binky looked at each other. "Not me," they said together.

"**Definite**ly not me," said Arthur.

"Well, I don't want to be first," said Muffy. "I know . . . We could **spin** the diary around like a **compass**. When it stopped, the top would **point** to one of us. That person would have to open it."

"Sounds **fair**," said Francine.

"Yes," agreed Binky.

"Very," said Arthur.

"So, should we spin?" asked Muffy.

"NOOOO!" everyone else shouted.

"Maybe we could just stand it on end," said Francine. "Maybe it would fall over and open."

"That would almost be an **accident**," said

Muffy. "I like it."

They placed the diary **upright**.

"It looks **wobbly**," said Francine.

"Wobbly is good," Binky agreed.

The diary may have looked wobbly, but it didn't move.

"Maybe we're not **staring** hard enough," said Muffy.

Francine **blink**ed. "I can't stare any harder. I'm getting **cross-eyed**."

"What if a strong wind came in and **knock**ed the diary open?" said Muffy.

"Yeah," said Francine. "And that same wind might **flip** the pages. . . ."

They waited **patient**ly for a wind to **come by**. They waited and waited.

"Muffy, what are you doing?" asked Arthur.

Muffy **blush**ed. "Me? Nothing."

"There! You did it again." Arthur pointed a finger at her. "You're **blow**ing at the book."

"Don't be **silly**," said Muffy. "I'm just, um, doing some **breathing exercise**s."

Binky **snort**ed. "Well, you're going to have to breathe a lot harder if you want to get anywhere."

He **let out** a very deep **breath**.

"And what was that?" asked Arthur.

"Just a **sigh**, Arthur," said Francine. "You can't **blame** Binky for sighing. I think a little sigh would do me some good."

Arthur **cross**ed his arms. "Now you're all **huff**ing **and puff**ing. It's not right."

"I have to agree with Arthur," said Binky. "I don't think the wind is going to be enough. What we need is an **earthquake**."

"Not much chance of that," said Arthur.

"You never know," said Binky, kicking the table hard.

The book fell over—but it was still shut.

"Hey!" said Arthur. "That's **cheat**ing."

"It was just an **experiment**," Binky **insist**ed.

My
Diary
PRIVATE
Do NOT Open

"I wanted to see if an earthquake would help."

"Forget the wind and the earthquake," said Francine. "Maybe we should just all read it together. That way we'll all be **equal**ly . . . **guilty**."

Nobody could **argue** with that.

Chapter 9

"My whole life is in that diary!" said Sue Ellen.

"I'm sure it is," said Ms. Turner. She had taken Sue Ellen into the **staff** room to **console** her.

Sue Ellen **sigh**ed. "And now my whole life is gone."

"There, there, dear. You still have your life, **after all**. As for your diary, I'm sure it will **turn up**. Diaries don't just **vanish into thin air**."

"I've had that diary ever since I was six. I started it on the first day of first grade."

"Really," said Ms. Turner.

"That was my very first whole day of school.

I had never been in school that long before. When I got home, my mother helped me write down everything about it."

Ms. Turner **nod**ded.

"We started with Circle Time.★ I had a hard time sitting still. And I remember **staring** at another little girl because I had never seen anyone so **dress**ed **up**. Then the teacher read us a story. 'The Three Bears,✳' I think. I kept calling out for Goldilocks✲ to be careful, but I remember feeling sorry for the bears at the end. At least I think I did. I'd have to check in my—" Sue Ellen **bit** her lip. "But I can't check it, can I?"

Ms. Turner stood up and **rub**bed her hands

★ **Circle Time** 이야기 나누기 활동. 아이들이 둥그렇게 모여 앉아서 차례대로 이야기를 하거나 다같이 노래를 부르는 것을 말한다.

✳ **The Three Bears** '곰 세 마리 이야기'라는 영국의 전래동화. 골디락스라는 소녀가 어느 날 숲에서 길을 잃었다가 세 마리의 곰이 사는 오두막에 들어가면서 벌어지는 이야기를 담고 있다.

✲ **Goldilocks** 골디락스. '곰 세 마리 이야기'에 등장하는 소녀의 이름으로 'gold(금)'와 'lock(머리카락)' 두 단어가 합쳐진 말로 금발을 뜻한다.

together. "You know, maybe instead of sitting here, we'd **be better off** continuing the **hunt**."

"What if someone else finds it first?"

Ms. Turner **pat**ted Sue Ellen on the shoulder. "Then they'll **turn** it **in** at the desk, and all will be well."

Sue Ellen shook her head. "But what if that person reads the diary before returning it? No one **besides** me has ever read it."

"Now, Sue Ellen, I think you're getting yourself upset over nothing. You told me it says PRIVATE in big **letter**s right where everyone can see it."

"That's true," Sue Ellen **admit**ted.

"Why,* then, you have nothing to worry about."

"Sue Ellen!"

Arthur and the others were coming toward her.

★ **why** 이유를 묻거나 말할 때 쓰는 의문사 또는 관계사가 아닌 '그럼', '어머', 또는 '아니'라는 뜻의 감탄사로 쓰였다.

TOLON
STAFF
ROOM

"We have something for you," said Arthur. He held out the diary.

Sue Ellen **gasp**ed. "Where did you find it?" She took the diary and **hug**ged it against her **chest**.

"On one of the **cart**s," said Arthur. "I was going to give it right back to you—"

"But we stopped him," said Muffy.

"Because we wanted to look inside," Francine added.

"You did?" Sue Ellen hugged the diary tighter. "But it's PRIVATE. It says so right on the **cover**."

"Don't worry," said Arthur. "We didn't look."

"Even though we were **tempt**ed by winds and **earthquake**s," said Binky.

Sue Ellen didn't understand, but she smiled anyway. "Well, whatever the reason, thank you. And even though I'm breaking one of my **rule**s, I can tell you what I'm going to write tonight."

"What's that?" asked Binky.

Sue Ellen smiled. "That I have the best friends in the world."

As Sue Ellen was leaving the library, Binky held open the door for her.

"**Allow me**," he said.

Sue Ellen looked surprised. "Why, Binky, I didn't know you were such a gentleman."

"I'm not! That is, well, not usually." He looked at the ground. "And if you tell anyone, I'll **deny** it."

Sue Ellen smiled. "Don't worry. Your secret is safe with me."

She continued on to the bike **rack**, where Muffy was just getting ready to leave.

"See you later, Sue Ellen." Muffy put her foot on the **pedal**—and then stopped. "**By the way**, I'll be home tonight if you need any ideas for stories."

"Stories?"

"You know, something about a beautiful, rich, and **resourceful** princess saving the world."

"Oh. Thank you, Muffy. If that **come**s **up**, I'll give you a call."

Muffy **nod**ded and **rode** off.

"Oh, Sue Ellen," said Francine, running up behind her, "let me hold your books while you un**lock** your bike. Wouldn't want you to get hurt!"

"Um, thanks."

"Is there anything else I can help you with? I'm very **friendly**, you know. And **considerate**, too. And have I **mention**ed *nice?* Being nice is my best thing."

Sue Ellen looked **confuse**d.

"Well, see you tomorrow," said Francine. "Call me if you have any problems with your homework or if you just want to talk. And happy writing!"

Sue Ellen shook her head as she put on her bike helmet. She would never have **expect**ed that writing a diary would make her so popular.

She was still thinking about this as Arthur came out of the library.

"Arthur, are you sure nobody read my diary?" she asked.

"Don't worry, Sue Ellen. It's still **private**." He **paused**. "Is there anything else you want to ask me? Or maybe tell me?"

"I don't think so."

"You know, I take **criticism** really well. And I'm always ready to **improve** myself. So don't **hold back**."

Sue Ellen got on her bike. "I won't. You're sure about the diary. . . ."

MY
Diary
Private
DO NOT OPEN

"**Positive**."

"That's good. You might have been **embarrass**ed."

"Me?" Arthur **blink**ed. "I **suppose** you've written down a lot of ways I could improve."

Sue Ellen looked **puzzle**d. "No. Actually, I said some pretty nice things about you."

Arthur **blush**ed. "Really? Like what?"

"Sorry. My lips are **seal**ed."

Arthur **frown**ed. "That's not **fair**!"

"See you later!" said Sue Ellen, riding off.

"All right," Arthur called after her. "**In that case**, I'm going to start a diary of my own."

Sue Ellen **screech**ed to a stop.

"You are? What are you going to **put in** it?"

Arthur smiled. "That," he said, "will be my little secret."